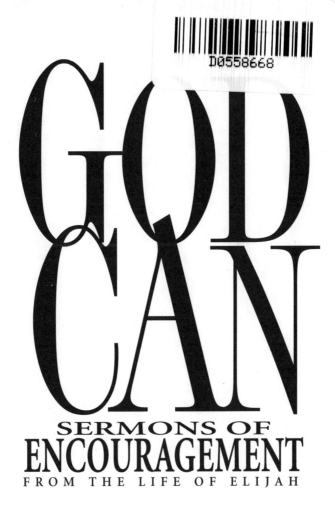

GOD CAN

SERMONS OF
ENCOURAGEMENT
FROM THE LIFE OF ELIJAH

Bishop John R. Bryant

GOD CAN

SERMONS OF
ENCOURAGEMENT
FROM THE LIFE OF ELIJAH

Helping Hands

Helping Hands Press
P.O. Box 133 • Keene, TX 76059 • Phone (817) 645-3258

For book orders contact:
BISHOP JOHN MINISTRIES
4347 South Hampton Road, Suite 245 • Dallas, TX 75232
Phone (214) 333-2632 • FAX (214) 333-1960

For book orders contact:

Bishop John Ministries
4347 South Hampton Rd., Suite 245
Dallas, Texas 75232
Telephone: 214-333-2632
FAX: 214-333-1960

Edited by Roland J. Hill

Editioral Assistance: Susie Hill, Daryl Ingram, Marcus Sheffield, MaryAnn Hadley

Cover art direction & design: Ed Guthero

Cover texture art: Jerri Desmond

Book Design and Layout by TypeRight Graphics, Grand Rapids, Michigan

Helping Hands Press, P.O. Box 133, Keene, Texas, 76059   817-645-3258

ISBN: 1-889390-01-1

DEDICATION

To the memory of my dear parents
Bishop Harrison Bryant
and
Mother Edith Holland Bryant

In honor of my living parent
Mother Pauline Williams

CONTENTS

ACKNOWLEDGEMENTS

I want to first give thanks to my Lord and Savior Jesus Christ, for it is by His grace that this project has been completed. I am so thankful for the beautiful people the Lord raised up to help me. Cassandra Trigg typed the first draft from my handwritten manuscript; considering my handwriting, that was a miracle in itself. Dr. Vivian Davis did the line editing, for which I am grateful. Dr. Lee Monroe, president of Paul Quinn College, freed up two members of his staff, Gloria Richard and Beverly Smith, who did a wonderful job with manuscript preparation.

I am one of those persons who from time to time needs to be motivated to keep pushing. I thank God for Dr. William Watley who kept me encouraged and Dr. Roland J. Hill for stepping in at the eleventh hour to edit and pull this whole project together, proving that "God Can." Finally, I thank God for my family, my wife, the Rev. Cecelia Williams Bryant, and my son and daughter, Rev. Jamal Harrison and Thema Simone, who continue to back me up in all my endeavors.

INTRODUCTION

It seems that as we move into a new millienuun, more than at any time before, the human landscape is dotted with skyscrapers of fear, pain, frustration, and anxiety. This malady is not confined to any one race, gender, generation, or class. The forebodings are in every neighborhood in the land. Cynicism, pessimism, and hopelessness are growing in this nation.

Though there exists a great concentration on self, more and more people do not seem to know who they are, or in whom or what they believe. A growing number of people doubt that they can experience true quality of life. Still many more individuals are committing or contemplating suicide. Abuses of alcohol, drugs and even food are on the increase. These dead-end avenues are being explored in the attempt to find pleasure and/or numb the senses against pain.

The causes of the pain, fear, frustration, and anxiety are varied. Topping the list is the war between the sexes, the changing roles of male and female, and the astonishing increase in divorce. One third of all children now live in single parent homes compounding the pain, fear, and frustration that covers this country. In this land of plenty there is a growing fear around economic issues. Real wages of all American workers have been in decline since 1973. Nearly twenty percent of the income of workers has eroded while the rich continue to get richer. People no longer feel secure about their jobs. There is growing uncertainty and anxiety about this country's economic future. America is also frustrated on its political front. This is apparent by the fewer citizens exercising their right to vote. More individuals are throwing up their hands and asking, "What's the use?" The nation seems to feel it cannot trust its political leaders. Fear of escalating crime rates has led many states, including Texas, to pass legislation which grants citizens the right to carry concealed weapons. In the Dallas/Forth Worth Metroplex, eleven thousand gun licenses were issued during the first three months after the law was passed in the state. Of the eleven thousand gun licenses issued, over nine thousand went to white males. It seems as if white males are the most frightened.

Our military and our police forces are the best equipped in the world; our private citizenry is the most armed, yet fear persists throughout the land. This nation is in trouble from "sea to shining sea." Our whole nation cries for help.

If the entire nation is in trouble and in need of help, then what about those on the bottom rung of the economic, political, and social ladder? It has been said that when America catches a cold, the African-American comes down with pneumonia. Cornel West, in his book, *Race Matters*, estimates that one in every five children in this country lives in poverty. The figure worsens with African-Americans. One in every two black children lives below the poverty line. You know our country is in trouble when half of America's children live in female headed homes without any safety net to catch them.

In a capitalistic culture where material possessions define self-worth, one seems almost justified in acquiring those possessions by any means necessary. For those who are denied an equal opportunity, crime, as often as not, becomes the means of acquisition.

Kweisi Mfume stated in his "State of Black America" speech, at the Congressional Black Caucus weekend in 1994, "One of the worst problems we face today is the horror of crime. It has gripped our cities in terror and has changed our lives in a very real and sobering way. We have become manifestations of both fear and frustration—physically, mentally, and even economically."

The larger society responds to crime by hiring more police and building more prisons, while what is needed is job training that leads to viable employment. The government intends to limit the welfare programs, but proposes no sufficient job programs to put in their place. Politicians seem intent on destroying Affirmative Action programs even though the African-American community is well aware that racism still prevents the masses of Blacks from a fair chance at climbing up from the bottom. And so all across this land rage, despair, and hopelessness grows. We can see this rage in a dramatic way among young unemployed African-Americans.

An old hymn asks the question, "Is there anyone can help us?"

I am convinced that God Can.

The narratives in I Kings 17 & 18 provide marvelous examples of the lengths to which God is willing and able to go on behalf of the believer who turns to Him. As you study these passages with me, it is my hope that you will discover, as I have, our greatest resource for liberation, empowerment, and reconciliation. I hope you will come to believe, as I have, that God Can.

It is my prayer that as you mediate on these sermons that they will bring you encouragement. If there is any area in which you personally have given up, I am praying that you will come to the conviction that no situation or problem is too great that God cannot provide whatever you need to be victorious. My intention is to convince you that God Can " do exceeding abundantly above all that we ask or think." (Ephesians 3:20)

PROLOGUE

IS THERE ANYONE CAN HELP US?

Is there anyone can help us, one who understands
  our hearts,
When the thorns of life have pierced them till they
  bleed;
One who sympathizes with us, who in wondrous
  love imparts
Just the very, very blessing that we need?

Is there anyone can help us who the load is hard
  to bear,
And we faint and fall beneath it in alarm;
Who in tenderness will lift, and the heavy burden
  share,
And support us with an everlasting arm?

Is there anyone can help us who can give a sinner
  peace,
When his heart is burdened down with pain and
  woe;

Who can speak the word of pardon that affords a
　　sweet release,
And whose blood can wash and make us like the
　　snow?

Is there anyone can help us when the end is draw-
　　ing near,
Who will go through death's dark waters by our
　　side;
Who will light the way before us, and dispel all
　　doubt and fear,
And will bear our spirits safely o'er the tide?

Refrain

Yes, there's one, God Can
Yes, there's one, God Can
The blessed, blessed Jesus, He's the one;
When afflictions press the soul,
When waves of trouble roll,
And you need a friend to help you,
God Can! *

* Mackay, J.B. " Is There Anyone Can Help Us?" *AMEC Bicentennial
Hymnal*; The African Methodist Episcopal Church, 1984.

GOD CAN
Back You Up

And Elijah the Tisbite, who was of the inhabitants of Gilead, said unto Ahab, as the Lord God of Israel liveth, before whom I stand, there shall not be dew nor rain these years, but according to my word.

—*I Kings 17:1*

GOD CAN
Back You Up

H ave you ever been in a difficult situation and felt you were completely on your own? You faced a problem, a concern, a condition that was tough. You knew you needed some help; but somehow you were convinced there was no help available. Perhaps that is what the African slaves in America must have been experiencing when they sang, "Way down yonder by myself, and I couldn't hear nobody pray." The blues singer expressed this same sentiment when he moaned, "Don't nobody love me, don't nobody even care!"

Have you been there? Have you been in that difficult place where it seemed no one had your back? Have you felt completely alone, unprotected, on your own—vulnerable? Maybe as you read this book, right now, you're experiencing those feelings of abandonment. If so, I want you to know that I have prayed and am praying that the words that follow will minister to you. I am aware that when you face difficulties, and the feelings of loneliness crowd in, this is no light matter. Such feelings can create fear, distort reality, chip away at your faith, and make you feel defeated before you have even entered the battle.

It was the feeling of aloneness that drove the prophet Elijah to hide in a cave. Even the prophet of God felt, at times, all by himself. Fear distorted reality and God had to remind him:

"And the Lord said unto him, Go, return on thy way to the wilderness of Damascus: and when thou comest, anoint Hazael to be king over Syria: And Jehu the son of Nimshi shalt thou anoint to be king over Israel: and Elisha the son of Shaphat of Abel-meholah shalt thou anoint to be prophet in thy room. And it shall come to pass, that him that escapeth the sword of Hazael shall Jehu slay: and him that escapeth from the sword of Jehu shall Elisha slay. Yet I have left seven thousand in Israel, all the knees which have not bowed unto Baal, and every mouth which hath not kissed him." (I Kings 19:14-18)

Feelings of isolation that go unchecked can drive a person into a deep hole of depression. Such feelings have been known to drive many persons to drink, to drugs, and even to eating disorders. Aloneness can impel us into hiding in many different kinds of caves. You can find yourself hiding in the cave of a bad relationship, feeling that "anybody is better than nobody." Caught in your cave of aloneness, you decide to just "make do." Young people deal with their aloneness in the cave of gangs. When the family becomes dysfunctional; father may be gone, mother may be tired, angry, hurt, depressed, and the child is hungry for family. Gangs call out, "Come join us; we will be your family. You don't have to be alone. If you are with us, we'll have your back."

You may not be in a gang; you may not be abusing drugs. But I suspect that the fear of being alone has driven many into fraternities, sororities, social clubs, and other organizations. Some have even retreated into the cave of marriage to escape their aloneness. What cave are you hiding in?

I submit to you that there is hardly anyone who does not desire the confidence, the security, the comfort, the assurance, the boldness, the authority that comes when you know there is someone or something that will back you up.

Elijah clearly makes this point in his bold utterance to Ahab, the King of Israel:

"And Elijah the Tisbite, who was of the inhabitants of Gilead, said unto Ahab, As the Lord God of Israel liveth, before whom I stand, there shall not be dew nor rain these years, but according to my word." (I Kings 17:1)

Can you believe it? A country preacher confronting the King. Elijah is from Tishbe, that rugged, unsettled, half-civilized place in Gilead just east of Jordan. What right does he have speaking to the King in this way?

There are those who gain confidence from where they were born and raised. But not Elijah. How could you be proud of Tishbe. You would compare Tishbe to Nazareth of which it was asked, "Can there any good thing come out of Nazareth?" (John 1:16)

Not only was Elijah from a remote place that was not even near a city of renown, but the man himself finished no great schools, nor did he study under any great scholar. Elijah is not even credited with writing anything. The authorship of I Kings is unclear. There are those who believe Jeremiah had something to do with writing this history. Others maintain that the writer is unknown, but that the writer did his work under King Josiah. One thing that all the scholars seem to be clear about is that Elijah was not the writer. Yet he is counted as one of the great prophets.

Elijah's greatness was rooted in his relationship with God. There are significant lessons to be learned from Elijah's relationship with God. E. G. White in her book, *Prophets and Kings*, writes that Elijah spent much time in his mountain retreat. In his mountain retreat, he discovered the blessings of solitude, of silence, of unmolested time with God.

In solitude there is the blessing of silence. Out of the womb of silence is birthed one's deepest thoughts. It is in silence that one is able to best hear, see, learn, and feel. The importance of silence is a lesson that is taught by the life of Jesus. "And after he had dismissed the crowds, he went up into the mountain by himself to pray." (Matthew 14:2,3) Remember that a man or woman who is never silent has very little of consequence to say.

Elijah, in the silence of his mountain retreat, observed Israel descending deeper and deeper into idolatry. He watched them growing further away from the "one true and living God." Idolatry is the act of putting anyone or anything in God's place. And Elijah's heart broke as he witnessed his people turn from the true and living God to the worship of the idol god-Baal. God had given Israel the "land of promise."

"Go, and gather the elders of Israel together, and say unto them, The Lord God of your fathers, the God of Abraham, of Isaac, and Jacob, appeared unto me, saying, I have surely visited you, and seen that which is done to you in Egypt. And I have said, I will bring you up out of the affliction of Egypt unto the land of the Canaanites, and the Hittites, and the Amorites, and the Perizzites, and the Hivites, and the Jebusites, unto a land flowing with milk and honey." (Exodus 3:15,16)

"And the Lord said unto Moses, Depart, and go up hence, thou and the people which thou hast brought up out of the land of Egypt, unto the land which I sware unto Abraham, to Isaac, and to Jacob, saying, Unto thy seed will I give it: And I will send an angel before thee; and I will drive out the Canaanite, the Amorite, and the Hittite, and the Perizzite, the Hivite, and the Jebusites; Unto a land flowing with milk and honey. . ." (Exodus 33:1-3)

In giving them the promised land, God was also giving Israel the promise of victory over their enemies. God kept His word. The enemy was defeated.

But Israel responded by turning to the gods of their enemies and not the God of their victory.

I find it very strange that people today will adopt the styles, the attitudes, the values, and the beliefs of those who are in opposition to their advancement. Many of us treat our enemies with more respect than we treat our friends.

Elijah did not like the way Israel was disrespecting God. To be over-looked, put-down, treated discourteously and rudely is considered by most of us as unacceptable behavior. Some young African-Americans claim that to be "dissed" (disrespected) is reason to fight. And to be sure, none of us want to be disrespected. But in our society we observe more and more instances of persons disrespecting others.

It is bad to watch people disrespect their own people. African-Americans, who have accepted others' negative definitions of who African-Americans are, will treat white Americans with respect, but are unable to give respect to their own.

I have observed, with alarm, the growing disrespect many children show their parents. The same disrespect can be observed between many husbands and wives. But when one disrespects one's self, it is almost impossible for one to respect anyone else. Individuals who do not appreciate their own lives or value their own minds and bodies end up having a distorted view of the Creator. They wind up disrespecting God.

Elijah could no longer stomach creatures who disrespected the Creator. So he prayed that something drastic would happened that would lead the Hebrews back to God. Sometimes it takes something drastic in our lives to make us face the reality that we need God. When the marriage gets in serious trouble, when sickness forces us into a hospital stay, when we have to face a judge and a court room, when we are in dire straits, that's when many of us begin looking for God. I know I was forced to look for God several years ago while doing renovations on the church I was pastoring in Baltimore, Maryland, the Bethel A.M.E. Church.

During the renovation project, we held services in a rented facility. Everything was going as planned, and I thought to myself "This job is pretty easy." The membership was growing rapidly, and the faithfulness of the saints in raising money for the project allowed us to service the bank loan without any problem. Who would have suspected any trouble ahead? But all of a sudden trouble broke out all around us. What could go wrong—did go wrong. It was during that trouble I realized that I was part of the problem. Because things were going so smoothly, I had taken God for granted. I had not invited Him to take charge of the job. Immediately, I called the church into a season of prayer and fasting. "Howbeit, this kind goeth not out but by prayer and fasting." (Matthew 17:21) Sometimes difficulty has to come into our lives in order for God to get our attention. It took something drastic in the life of Bethel before we turned to the Lord.

When Elijah prayed for something drastic to turn Israel back to God, God heard his prayer and shut the heavens. "Elijah was a man subject to like passions as we are, and he prayed earnestly that it might not rain: and it rained not on the earth by the space of three years and six months." (James 5:17) Elijah believed God completely. Someone might ask, "How do you know he believed God completely?" I know he believed God because he "went public." "And Elijah the Tishbite, who was of the inhabitants of Gilead, said unto Ahab, As the Lord God of Israel liveth, before who I stand, there shall not be dew nor rain these years, but according to my word." (I Kings 17:1) Elijah knew that God would back him up.

Visualize Elijah as he stands before King Ahab with authority, boldness, and confidence. Elijah said to the king, "As the Lord God of Israel liveth, there will be no rain." As he liveth—that my brothers and sisters is the key. One needs a living God to back you up. The Baals of this world cannot back you up. Dead, inanimate, artificial, false, material stuff cannot support and undergird you. You need a living God to back you up.

Elijah had some strong reasons for believing that God would back him up. The prophet knew without doubt that God would back up His own Word. There is a lifetime guarantee on God's Word. "Heaven and earth shall pass away, but my words shall not pass." (Matthew 24:35) James 5:17 tells us that God, by His spirit, told Elijah to pray that there would be no rain. When the prophet speaks, E. G. White says he does not speak as the master but as the minister. God is the master; He is the author. The believer's task is to make sure that his walking and talking is in obedience to Him. When the believer lines up with the will of God, then God will back him up. God acts in response to the believer's faith and trust in Him.

Elijah's faith was an outgrowth of his prayer life. Prayer is more than talking to God. Powerful prayer occurs when God talks back. Too many of us do not pray long enough. We do all the talking, then we are finished. God is looking for believers who will wait long enough to hear His voice. "To him the porter openeth, and the sheep hear his voice: and He calleth his own sheep by name, and leadeth them out." (John 10:3) The believer who is lined up with the word of God, needs to pray in faith until he hears the Lord say, "I've got you covered; I've got your back. I'll back you up."

Finally, the Lord backed up Elijah because he stood for his God when others had forsakened Him. Elijah stood for the Lord because he was able to experience a revelation of God's presence. Throughout the 17th and 18th chapters of I Kings, one is able to read of the intimate relationship between the prophet and his God.

The believer must press to reach a level of intimacy with the Lord. Every believer must make reaching a high level of intimacy with God the focus of his or her prayer life. You must determine that worship, praise, and intimacy with the Creator will be your major goal.

Because many in Israel did not press for this intimacy, they were unable to encounter or see God.

Therefore, they wound up choosing to follow what they could see—Baal. Has your lack of intimacy with God led you to follow Baal?

People tend to call on, depend on, count on, trust in what they can see and handle. That is the reason so many call on "homemade" gods—the Baal gods. In fact, many have turned their houses, cars, jewelry, educational degrees, bank accounts, husbands or wives into modern-day Baals.

Take a few moments to reflect. Are there any idols in your life that need to be torn down? In West Africa, there is a praise song that calls all political and material gods "powerless powers." Do you have "powerless powers" in your life? As we move into a new millienuun and disparities become greater among people, we need a powerful God. In a nation where plenty is afforded a few and poverty is the lot of many, we need the power of God. In an age of technological advances where people know more and have more and yet they are still hopeless, we need to encounter the power of God.

I want you to know that having an encounter with God is a guarantee of a victorious life no matter what the circumstances. You can be assured that help and support will always be available as long as you are in a relationship with God. Understand that the help you need to back you up is not in yourself. It is not in any man-made entity. It is only found in a relationship with the living God. No matter the severity of what you are facing, know that when you can see God and call on the Lord in faith, He will back you up.

Through the agony of Calvary, Jesus saw God. While others at the cross heard Jesus talking, they couldn't see what He saw. I imagine they thought He was only talking to His mother, or maybe death, or maybe the two thieves that hung next to Him, or maybe to pain or defeat. They couldn't see God, so they drew the wrong conclusions. No, Jesus was not talking to any earthly concerns, He was talking to His father. And so He cried out, "Father into thy hands I commend my spirit." (Luke 23:46) And Jesus died.

But Matthew, Mark, Luke, and John all proclaim that early on the third day morning the Life-Giver backed him up. Jesus had declared, "Destroy this temple, and in three days I will raise it up." (John 2:19) Jesus knew His Father would back Him up. Like Elijah, He completely trusted in His Father.

I want you to know that the Lord will back you up. No matter what you are going through, if you are in a relationship with him, you will never be alone. He is there with you. He does see you. He does care about you. So if you are in a courtroom, on a rough job, on a hospital operating table, in a bad marriage, or struggling to raise those children, God will back you up. Trust God. David did! Listen to his confident declaration, "Surely goodness and mercy shall follow me all the days of my life: and I will dwell in the house of the Lord forever." (Psalms 23:6) Paul also knew that the Lord will back you up. It was evident when he wrote these words to his Philippian friends, "I can do all

things through Christ which strengtheneth me."
(Philippians 4:13)

Dear reader, to you, I say—Be Encouraged!
God Can Back You Up!

GOD CAN
Use Anything

And the word of the Lord came unto him saying, get thee hence, and turn thee eastward, and hide thyself by the brook Cherith, that is before Jordan. And it shall be, that thou shalt drink of the brook; and I have commanded the ravens to feed thee there. So he went and did according unto the word of the Lord: for he went and dwelt by the brook Cherith, that is before Jordan. And the ravens brought him bread and flesh in the morning, and bread and flesh in the evenings; and he drank of the brook.

—I Kings 17:2-6

GOD CAN
Use Anything

God sends the prophet Elijah to a hiding place down by the brook Cherith. Why does God do this? I believe it was not only to protect Elijah from his enemies, but to give believers two important lessons about His abilities. I believe God wants us to know that He can. The first lesson to be learned from Elijah's brook experience is that God can provide a hiding place. "For in the time of trouble He shall hide me in His pavilion: in the secret of His tabernacle shall He hide me; He shall set me upon a rock." (Psalms 27:5) "Thou shalt hide them in the secret of thy presence from the pride of man: Thou shalt keep them secretly in a pavilion from the strife of tongues." (Psalms 31:20)

When you decide to follow the Lord, you must accept the fact that He will lead you to some demanding places. The Lord will lead you to places of service. He will lead you to places of war and places of struggle. In some of those places you will encounter ingratitude.

Some of the places will be dangerous, and some will be demon dominated. He will not always lead you beside still waters. As much as some of us would like it, the Lord will not simply let us find a place on a comfortable pew or pulpit. No, God calls us, from time to time to some dangerous, demanding, and draining places. And since He does lead us into some precarious situations, every now and then He calls us out of those places into a hiding place. But notice this, God knows not only how to provide a hiding place, but He knows when to hide us. What assurance!

The life of Jesus is a testimony to kingdom timing. It was apparent throughout the life of Christ that God is the master of the time and place of hiding. "Then took they up stones to cast at him: but Jesus hid Himself, and went out of the temple, going through the midst of them and so passed by." (John 8:59) "Therefore they sought again to take him: but he escaped out of their hand, and went away again beyond Jordan in the place where John at first baptized: and there he abode." (John 10:39,40) Yes, God knows where to hide us and when to hide us. This is good news in this technically advanced age where emotional stress and strain have taken their toll. This is good news for the many struggling to avoid "burn-out" and "breakdown."

There is a need for that place where one can just commune with the Lord. In the African-American church there was a song I heard often when I was a boy,

"Have a little talk with Jesus;
Tell Him all about our troubles.
He will hear our faintest cry
And answer by and by
You feel a little prayer wheel turning
Know a little fire is burning
Just have a little talk with Jesus
Makes it right–all right."

Over and over again Jesus slipped away to be with His Father. He would go alone into the mountains to talk with the Lord. It is obvious that He saw his own need in those moments of communion. We must know that if Jesus, the Son of God, our sinless Lord, needed a hiding place to commune with God, how much more do we sinful human beings need that hiding place in God.

We live in a dangerous world-on an explosive planet. A hiding place is essential for our safety. There are times when we need spiritual, psychological, and even physical safety. It's comforting to know our God can hide us.

Elijah needed a hiding place, a safe haven to protect him from his enemies. Because of Israel's sin, Elijah had gone to King Ahab and announced that there would be no rain. I imagine that initially they just laughed at Elijah. They probably said among themselves, "It was only last week when it rained. The rivers are full; the ground is moist; the flowers are in full bloom; the crops are plenteous; the livestock have plenty to eat and drink. This prophecy of Elijah is a joke."

Perhaps Elijah was laughed at as Noah was laughed at when he built that boat on dry ground and declared, "It's going to rain." They probably laughed at Elijah like some will laugh at you when you tell them to get right with God.

But when days turned to weeks, weeks into months, and months into years, and there was no rain, their laughter turned to anger. They became angry, not with themselves because of their sins, but with Elijah, God's messenger. They wanted to punish Elijah for his painful decree, and would have, had not God provided him a hiding place. When people do not like the message, they have a way of turning on the messenger. This attitude almost resulted in Jeremiah walking away from his ministry. And it has tempted many preachers to preach a "watered down" gospel.

The Lord, our God, is Jehovah Jireh-God our provider. He provided Elijah a hiding place. But He didn't stop there. He met Elijah's needs while in that hiding place. Sometimes when God attempts to separate us for a season of rest, protection, and restoration, we refuse because we feel that we must remain in the eye of the storm in order to provide for ourselves the day-to-day necessities. We fail to believe that not only can God provide a hiding place, but he can provide all our needs in that hiding place. "But my God shall supply all your need according to his riches in glory by Christ Jesus." (Philippian 4:19)

While Elijah was in his hiding place, God gave him this message of assurance, "And it shall be that thou shalt drink of the brook; and I have commanded the ravens to feed thee there." (I Kings 17:4)

Elijah discovered that even in a drought God can make a way! In verse 4, Elijah learned his second lesson that God can use anything to fulfill His promise. God commanded the ravens to feed Elijah in his hiding place. It's good to know God can use anything. God is in charge! No matter what foe you are facing, believe that God is in charge!

God said in that same verse 4, "I command." That is the kind of God we serve—a God who has the power to command. You must remind yourself that "the earth is the Lord's and the fullness thereof, the world, and they that dwell therein. For he hath founded it upon the seas, and established it upon the floods." (Psalms 24:1, 2) Since it is His world by creation, God can use anything in the world to do His will. In the book of Genesis, He told a ram to get in Abraham's bush.

"And Abraham lifted up his eyes, and looked, and behold behind him a ram caught in a thicket by his horns: and Abraham went and took the ram, and offered him up for a burnt offering in the stead of his son." (Genesis 22:13)

In II Kings, he used two she bears.

"And he (Elisha) went up from thence unto Bethel: and as he was going up by the way, there came forth little children out of the city, and mocked him, and said unto him, Go up, thou bald head, go up, thou bald head. And he turned back, and looked on them, and cursed them in the name of the Lord. And there came forth two she bears out of the wood, and tore forty and two children of them." (II Kings 2:23, 24)

In Daniel 6, He directed lions to go on a fast.

"My God hath sent his angels, and hath shut the lions' mouth, that they have not hurt me." (Daniel 6:22)

And in Numbers 22, God spoke through a jackass to get through to Balaam.

"And the ass said unto Balaam, Am not I thine ass, upon which thou has ridden ever since I was thine unto this day? Was I ever wont to do so unto thee? and he said, Nay." (Numbers 22:30)

And finally in this story, God commanded ravens to feed Elijah. God will use anything to do his will. This is what Elijah learned in his hiding place.

It is amazing that God commanded ravens to service his discouraged servant. Ravens are considered by the scripture to be "unclean birds" (Rev. 11:15; Deut. 14:14). Ravens were thought of not only as unclean birds but unhealthy for the body. They were birds of prey. Ravens were more likely to take food than to bring food. But when the Lord gets ready to bless you, He can use anything.

Some Bible scholars have heatedly debated the translation of the word "ravens" in I Kings 17:4. Some say that the "ravens" were not birds. They say the ravens were actually some Arabians, explaining that in the Hebrew language the word for "ravens" translates

"Arabians." Others say the ravens were in fact some merchants who fed Elijah, for "merchants" too can be translated "ravens." St. Jerome wrote that Elijah was in reality fed by the people of a small city called Orem. None of these interpretations contradict what I maintain. I maintain that God fed His prophet, and that He can use anything. The living God can use Arabians, merchants, citizens, or birds of prey. It doesn't matter which one you think it to be. The concept is still the same—God can use anything.

My wife, Cecelia (Rev. Cee), said on one occasion that "the very thing the Devil puts in your life to break you down, the Lord can use to build you up." You may not have grown up in a "Betty Crocker House." You may not have been raised by two loving and supportive parents. You may not have a Ph.D. You may not have more money than bills. You may not have political contacts downtown. But God doesn't need any of that to bless you. I tell you, without a doubt, God can use anything. He can use a school boy's lunch to feed a multitude. He can use a boy's sling shot to bring down a giant. He can use an old ex-slave woman, Harriet Tubman, on the Underground Railroad to set captives free. He can use a Georgia preacher, Martin Luther King, Jr., giving him nothing but a dream to stir a nation and the world. He can use an ex-convict, Nelson Mandela, after twenty-seven years in jail, making him head of the very nation that incarcerated him. He used a man with a thorn in the flesh, the apostle Paul, to pen more books in the New Testament than any other writer. Just remember, God can use anything and anybody.

But one of the greatest mysteries is that God is willing to use even Himself to save us. Sarah Hornsby in her book, *At the Name of Jesus*, states that, "Jesus is captor. He gave Himself to the forces of evil, taking on Himself all of our sins, sicknesses, and griefs. He entered hell, overcame Satan, and in triumph rose leading all who would join Him." What a God! He will use anything to rescue lost souls—even Himself.

Dear reader, as you go through the tough times of life, remember that God will provide a hiding place for you. But not only will He provide you a safe haven, He will use whatever it takes to provide for the needs of those that love Him and live according to His will. Please don't forget—God Can Use Anything.

GOD CAN
Multiply by Subtracting

And the word of the Lord came unto him, saying arise, get thee to Zarephath, which belongeth to Sidon and dwell there; behold, I have commanded a widow woman there to sustain thee. So he arose and went to Zarephath. And when he came to the gate of the city, behold, the widow woman was there gathering of sticks: and he called to her, and said, Bring me, I pray thee, a morsel of bread in thine hand. And she said, as the Lord thy God liveth, I have not a cake, but a handful of meal in a barrel, and a little oil in a cruse: and, behold, I am gathering two sticks, that I may go in and dress it for me and my son, that we may eat it, and die. And Elijah said unto her, Fear not; go and do as thou hast said: but make me thereof a little cake first, and bring it unto me, and after make for thee and for thy son. For thus said the Lord God of Israel, The barrel of meal shall not waste, neither shall the cruse of oil fail, until the day that the Lord sendeth rain upon the earth.

—*I Kings 17:8 -14*

GOD CAN
Multiply by Subtracting

We serve a mighty God! From time to time every believer needs to be reminded of this fact. Knowing that we serve a mighty God does help the believer face the trouble, pain, and struggle of every-day living.

Our world is in trouble with wars, human rights violations, famine, droughts, political corruption, debilitating poverty, and much more. And yet we need not be alarmed because we serve a mighty God.

African-American people continue to be confronted by challenges that loom like mountains before us. We must still overcome racism, a growing mean-spirited conservatism, substance abuse, gang violence, domestic violence, broken homes, teen parenting, self-hatred, and too often the death of hope. In almost every family someone is troubled by depression, addiction, divorce, AIDS, unemployment, loneliness, or sickness. But even in the face of all these problems, we must never forget that we serve a mighty God.

So we must be reminded that we serve a mighty God. Regularly, we must encourage ourselves with faith declarations:

"What God can't do, can't be done!"

"God can do anything but fail!"

"God can make a way out of no way!"

"God can bring life out of death, joy out of sorrow, and victory out of defeat!"

Some may think that these affirmations are only simplistic clichés, but they are significant because they testify of the power that brought us through the dark dungeon of slavery and the terror of segregation. They made us a nation when others plotted our genocide. As we make our sacrificial contributions to the world, these same religious maxims sustain us. These faith declarations affirm our power as children of the omnipotent God.

To do His work, the Lord uses different methods. In this chapter I want to highlight one of them. It is what I call—God's Mathematical Formula. It is a higher mathematical formula that only He can use.

God can multiply by subtracting!

I Kings 17:8-14, describes the Lord's use of this formula. Because Israel sinned against God, the clouds went on strike, and there was no rain. Elijah had prayed about Israel's sinful situation, and when he received affirmation, Elijah announced that the Lord would stop the rain. When the drought set in, King

Ahab, at the urging of his wife Jezebel, sent out a deputized search party. Their goal was to find the prophet and kill him. But the "can do" God had hidden His prophet.

In hiding, God provided Elijah's basic needs. He gave him water from the brook at Cherith and manna (food) was flown in twice a day. But soon the brook dried up. The drought had taken its toll. It is a fact that when the land is under judgment, everything, and everybody is affected—the believer and the non-believer as well. When prayer was removed from the classrooms of our nation, God did not like it and "turned His face." Because the prayer covering has been removed, our children must attend schools full of profanity, violence, extortion, drugs, rape, and even murder. When the judgment of God is in the land, everyone is affected.

The sin of the people of Israel caused God to stop the rain which caused even the prophet's brook to dry up. When the land is under judgment many suffer. I have seen some dried-up churches that have destroyed Christian families to the extent that even their love for each other is dried up. I have heard some dried-up sermons, and I have seen, even in God's church, a lot of dried-up lives. Preventing the kind of spiritual dryness that leads to such overwhelming consequences is one of the important reasons that the Christian church must work to cause the culture to submit to the will and way of the Lord.

Yet, even in the drought, Elijah kept his eyes on the Lord. Even though it was clear that the land was under jugdment, the man of God kept his eyes on his Lord. He could say like David, "But mine eyes are unto thee oh, Lord God: in thee is my trust; leave not my soul destitute." (Psalms 141:8) The God who can use anything sent His servant Elijah to a woman who had close to nothing, in order that she might give him everything he needed.

God directed Elijah to go to Zarephath to see a widow woman. He was told to ask from her what he needed. In essence, Elijah was told to take from her— Subtract. The women was in dire poverty, but it was from her the prophet was commanded to subtract. She had to feed him with next to nothing. But from this single parent, Elijah was directed by God to subtract.

Elijah found the woman at the gate of the city gathering cooking sticks. He asked her for some water and for something to eat. The woman answered by telling him that she was poor and that all she had was enough food to make one meal for her and her son. This is all she had, yet the holy man had the audacity to tell her to make a cake and bring it to him first. He had the audacity to ask her to do some subtraction.

This most assuredly was a major test of faith for the widow, for in verse 9, the Lord told Elijah that He had commanded the woman to feed him. Such a commandment would not be a test for the non-human part of God's creation, for all that part of creation obeys the Creator's commands. The sun rises; the seasons change; the birds sing; the winds and waves obey. Only God's human creatures have to decide whether or not to obey.

In the Bible, God commands believers to take responsibility, to love one another, to forgive those who offend, to worship Him in spirit and in truth. Nonetheless, we too often find it difficult to obey God. In all of creation, human beings too often stand in defiant disobedience against God. We usually have to determine how difficult it will be to obey, whether or not obedience will inconvenience us, or whether or not the command of God makes sense to us.

Let's put ourselves in the widow woman's place. She heard the voice of God speaking through the prophet. The command was clear.

But I can imagine that her flesh caused her to question whether or not that was the voice of God. We should have no difficulty thinking what she may have reasoned to herself: "God wouldn't ask me to do something that crazy. That's not God, girl. That's just the Devil trying to make a fool of you. You better look out for yourself and your son like you got good sense. Let someone else feed the prophet who can afford to because it's obvious you can't."

To the eye of flesh, subtraction looks like loss, it looks like defeat, it looks like you're being taken advantage of. But to the eyes of faith, subtraction looks like multiplication, it looks like victory. The widow's situation was indeed a test of her faith. The Lord was going to do what only he can do—multiply by subtracting. Our God is a giver. (John 3:16) To be His followers, we too must be givers. (Luke 6:38)

The window woman was poor, she was alone, she was hungry. God wanted to bless her, but He wanted her to demonstrate that she trusted Him enough to give. As poor as she was, she demonstrated that she was nonetheless willing to give—subtract. Then God began to multiply. The Bible says that she and her household could not exhaust their food supply while feeding the man of God.

It is still true of the kingdom of God; when you are willing to give your all, even your life, blessings will multiply for you in the kingdom. The Bible illustrates, through many examples, God's Multiplication Formula—God multiplies by subtracting. Just one example will demonstrate this higher math. Jesus subtracted a little boy's lunch, prayed over it, and multiplied it to feed five thousand. Now that's some math. But that's what God can do—God can multiply by subtracting.

When I was a boy, my parents made it a practice that whoever came to our door at meal time was fed. They ate right along with all the rest of us. Many times the meal looked as if it were sufficient only for the family, but my mother would cut and serve. Everyone ate, and no one left the table hungry. I call that heaven's mathematical formula in operation.

The Lord Jesus promised believes that they would not lose by giving. "Give, and it shall be given unto you; good measure, pressed down, and shaken together, and running over, shall men give into your bosom. For with the same measure that ye mete withal it shall be measured to you again." (Luke 6:38) The very word of God itself has multiplication power. His word multiplies faith. "So faith comes by hearing and hearing by the word of God." (Romans 10:17) God's word does not return void. "So shall my word be that goeth forth out of my mouth: it shall not return unto me void, but it shall accomplish that which I please, and it shall prosper in the thing whereto I sent it." (Isaiah 55:11) With His word he spoke the world into existence.

Faith in God has multiplication power. When it looks as if you are falling, in God you are rising. When it appears you are losing, in God you are winning. Even when it seems you are dying, in God you are living, not just for now but for eternity. Believe Jesus who declared, "I am the resurrection, and the life: he that believeth in me, though he were dead, yet shall he live: and whosoever liveth and believeth in me shall never die." (John 11:25, 26)

My brothers and sisters, if you are a believer, someone will lie on you—that's subtraction. Someone may cheat you—that's subtraction. Someone may unjustly take your job from you—that's subtraction. But just remember, those who take from you are helping God to bless you, for behind all the subtraction, there is God's multiplication.

In Christ Jesus, you will be able to sing.

"This joy I have, the world didn't give it to me:
the world didn't give it to me and
the world can't take it away."

GOD CAN
Bring Revival

And he stretched himself upon the child three times, and cried unto the Lord my God, I pray thee, let this child's soul come into him again. And the Lord heard the voice of Elijah; and the soul of the child came unto him again, and he revived.

—*I Kings 17:21, 22*

CHAPTER FOUR

GOD CAN
Bring Revival

The widow of Zarephath, showed great faith in God when she shared what she believed was her last meal with God's man, Elijah. In return, God multiplied her blessings in a supernatural way. The Lord promises great blessings to those who help the needy and support the work of the kingdom. Both the Old and New Testaments are full of references that compel believers to demonstrate a sense of mission to those who are in need.

In 1988, I was elected bishop in the African Methodist Episcopal Church and assigned to superintend our work in West Africa. How humbling it was to see Christians with so very little struggling with glad hearts as they did the work of the church. I wrote back to friends in the United States and gave them opportunities to support the churches in West Africa. I knew that the help from the American churches would not only be a blessing to the receivers, but also to the senders. The Bible promises, "Give, and it shall be given unto you; good measure, pressed down, and shaken together, and running over, shall men give into you bosom." (Luke 6:38) God's word also declares, "Cast thy bread upon the waters: for thou shalt find it after many days." (Ecclesiastes 11:1) In the book of Isaiah are these words that give assurance, "If thou draw out thy soul to the hungry, and satisfy the afflicted soul; then shall thy light rise in obscurity, and thy darkness be as the noonday: and the Lord shall guide thee continually, and satisfy thy soul in drought, and make fat thy bones; and thou shalt be like a watered garden, and like a spring of water, whose waters fail not." (Isaiah 58:10,11)

It seems to me that our nation has not taken these promises to heart. I am concerned at the nation's blatant disregard for the needs of the poor. It concerns me to hear so many voices clamoring to cut back on relief efforts for the poor. I am leery of this growing conservatism that is "mean-spirited." Too many of these persons see the poor, not as objects of mercy, but of scorn. They seem not to understand or believe that the God of the Bible still rewards the merciful. Can our nation expect to continue to experience the blessings of God while not following God's instructions?

The widow woman must have understood these promises because she had a spirit of sharing. And it was this spirit of sharing that allowed her and her household to eat during the drought. But this narrative of the widow woman doesn't end on a happy note. "After these things . . . ." (I Kings 17:17) That is, after the blessings, after the good times, after the miracles, the widow's son fell sick and died.

Some scholars have concluded that the son did not literally die, but slipped into a coma. I have no need to enter that particular debate. All I know is that the widow's son was in a very serious condition. This incident ought to remind us that you can be saved, spirit-filled, living holy, and in a good relationship with the Lord, and yet have trouble come into your life. Someone maybe asking, "If that is true, why give my life to Jesus Christ?" The answer is simple. You will go through tough times whether or not you give your heart to Christ. The difference is that when your troubled times come, the Lord can back you up. He can use anything to deliver you, including stepping into your subtraction in order to multiply your blessings.

But when trouble came into the widow's life, she did what so many of us do; she wanted to know- "Why?" "And she said unto Elijah, What have I to do with thee, O thou man of God? art thou come unto me to call my sin to remembrance, and to slay my son?" (I Kings 17:18)

Have you ever found yourself, in the midst of personal troubles, asking: "Why me? What did I do wrong? Am I being punished for something I've done wrong? Is this my fault?"

Elijah did not answer the woman's questions. Maybe he did not know the answers, but what he did know is clear. Elijah knew that God can bring revival. I can just hear the man of God as he may have said to this distraught mother,

"I don't know the answers to all your questions, but I know this—your son can be revived."

Do you need to be revived? Have the struggles, troubles, and stresses of life broken you down? Do you, or does someone close to you need revival? How about your marriage, your children, your friends, your church, our nation, do they need reviving? If so, keep your eyes on Elijah.

The first thing Elijah says to the widow is, "Give me your son." (I Kings 17:19) To bring revival, one must be willing to get involved. You cannot stand passively by. You must be willing to roll up your sleeves, work up a sweat, give your time, contribute your talent, give your money, cast your vote, and organize your block. As a matter of fact, when it comes to revival, the Lord will insist on your involvement. When Jesus Christ raised Lazarus from the dead, the Bible says He turned to those standing at the grave-site and directed them to "loose him, and let him go." (John 11:44) It is clear that if Jesus had enough power to raise a man from the dead, He certainly had sufficient power to take the death wrap from around him, but the Lord requires the believer's involvement.

An involved Elijah put the boy on his bed and stretched out on him. This act was symbolic of Elijah's willingness to give completely of himself. By getting involved, Elijah demonstrated his faith. So many Christians are not involved because they do not believe that they are or their church can really make a difference. Some Christians have given up on their communities, given up on so many of their young, given up on their people, given up on their own marriages, and even given up on themselves. But by getting involved Elijah demonstrated that he did not believe the situation was hopeless. He was saying, I know somebody who can bring revival to any and every seemingly dead situation or thing. Elijah's faith was born of his experiences with a "can do" God.

Have you had an experience with this "can do" God? In your life have there been times when God has entered a seemingly dead situation and brought life? When I look at African-American history, I am able to see the Lord, time and time again, making a way where there appeared to be no way. African-American history testifies to a God who can bring revival.

But involvement alone won't bring revival. Elijah began doing what really brings revival—praying. "And he cried unto the Lord, and said, O Lord my God, hast thou also brought evil upon the widow with whom I sojourn, by slaying her son?" (I Kings 17:20) If you want revival, remember that prayer is essential. Prayers of faith availeth much. "Ask, and it shall be given you; seek, and ye shall find; knock and it shall be opened unto you: For everyone that asketh receiveth; and he that seeketh findeth; and to him that knocketh it shall opened." (Matthew 7:7,8) Time and time again we see God responding to prayers of faith.

As he prayed, Elijah stretched out on the child three times, symbolic of his petition for help from the full council of God. Oh what power is available to the believer! The name of Jesus brings all the power of the Trinity to the disposal of the believer. It is the name of Jesus that is able to revive any dead situation or thing. God can bring revival.

Elijah wanted the widow's son revived from physical death, but I want you to know that a spiritual death is just as real. The person who is dying physically can no longer take into the body the nutrients that are necessary to sustain life. In like manner, any one who is experiencing spiritual death has no appetite for God's life-giving word, and no desire to do God's will. As an individual approaches physical death, the senses of hearing, taste, smell, seeing, and touch cease to function. Spiritual death likewise causes the loss of spiritual senses. One is unable to see the goodness of the Lord, or taste and see that the Lord is good. (Psalms 34:8) The individual who is dying spiritually finds it almost impossible to hear the word of the Lord. That person loses the capacity to feel the fire of God's Spirit.

The good news is God can bring revival wherever there is death. God can save that marriage. God can even raise one's self-esteem. God can deliver from drug addiction. God can save that son and daughter. God can help you put your house in order. God can raise a person up from stress, anxiety, and burn-out. God can liberate the African-American community. God can bring life back to your church and to your ministry. This "can do" God heard Elijah's prayer "and the soul of the child came unto him again, and he revived." (I Kings 17:22)

The Apostle Paul puts it this way: "So when this corruptible shall have put on incorruption, and this mortal shall have put on immortality, then shall be brought to pass the saying that is written, 'Death is swallowed up in victory. O death, where is thy sting? O grave, where is thy victory?' The sting of death is sin; and the strength of sin is the law. But thanks be to God, which giveth us victory through Jesus Christ." (I Corinthians 15:54-57)

The mothers and fathers of my tradition have testified that when the Lord revives you, you will be able to sing, "I looked at my hands, and they looked new. I look at my feet, and they did too." You will become a living testimony of the God who can bring revival.

GOD CAN
Light Your Fire

And Elijah came unto all the people and said, How long halt ye between two opinions? If the Lord be God, follow him: but if Baal, then follow him. And the people answered him not a word. Then said Elijah unto the people, I even I only remain a prophet of the Lord; but Baal's prophets are four hundred and fifty men. Let them therefore give us two bullocks; and let them choose one bullock for themselves, and cut it in pieces, and lay it on wood, and get no fire under: and I will dress the other bullock and lay it on wood, and put no fire under. And call ye on the name of your gods, and I will call on the name of the Lord: and the God that answereth by fire, let him be God. And all the people answered and said, it is well spoken.

—*I Kings 18:21-24*

GOD CAN
Light Your Fire

It had been three and a half years, and no rain had fallen. Everywhere one looked, there was evidence of a serious drought. Death had moved across the landscape with an unhindered march.

Initially, Elijah's weather forecast of no rain was ignored, but after months of no rain, King Ahab and his wife, Jezebel, became angry with God's prophet. In their anger they tried to hunt down Elijah in order it kill him, but the "can do" God had hidden him. When they were unable to find Elijah, their anger turned toward all the prophets of God. It became "open season" on those men of faith. Sometimes when I read the newspaper, look at television, or sit in a barber shop, where I am not known, I am able to witness a hostility on the part of many towards God's modern day prophets/preachers. Even in the African-American church, one witnesses a love-hate response to the humanity of the preacher.

When one pastor makes a mistake or demonstrates poor character, his or her fall is used by many to castigate all religious leaders. "Religious" folk have been doing that a long time, not realizing that in doing so, they are failing to walk after God's command. "Touch not my anointed, and do my prophets no harm." (Psalms 105:15)

After more than three years without rain, somebody in Israel was ready to listen to the Lord. And so I Kings 18 opens with evidence that there were some in Israel ready to listen and follow the way of the Lord. Some folks, it seemed, were moved by hard times to repent. Somebody was ready to "straighten up and fly right." Sometimes God has to cut off our rain, raise up a drought in our lives, and choke off our blessings in order to get our attention. There is nothing like trouble to move many of us to a season of repentance. Trouble can make people change their mind. The Prodigal Son is an excellent example of that truth. He left home with a distorted view of his father, but when tough times came, his mine changed about home and his father. The Bible said that trouble helped him "come to himself." (Luke 15:11ff)

Even though there was a readiness amongst some of the people, and even though God had the attention of some of them, Elijah knew he still had a fight on his hand. Real change does not come easily. The church needs to understand, every preacher needs to understand, and every believer needs to understand that when you are after minds and hearts for the kingdom, you must be prepared to fight. This is not the kind of stuff that Sunday afternoon teas and picnics are made of; this is warfare. Your opponent in this conflict is Satan, and he does not give up without a fight. God doesn't need any more church attenders. What He is looking for are warriors. He needs warriors who are prepared to march against Satan himself.

One of the things that makes Satan such a fierce opponent is that he is so cunning. He knows he cannot defeat the person who is connected to the Lord, so he works to keep the human soul disconnected from its Creator. Satan cannot force us out of a relationship with God. Through lies, the enemy will tempt you to make the decision to break off your relationship with God. Jesus' temptation in the wilderness illustrates Satan's deceptive tactics. Remember, Satan is the father of lies. He will lie about God. He will tell you God doesn't love you. He will tell you that God cannot save you. He will attempt to convince you that a substitute, artificial god is better than the real thing. He will offer you Baal: money, political power, fame, degrees, false religions. In West Africa there is a praise song in which these things are referred to as "powerless powers". The refrain of that song declares, however, that Jesus power is supernatural power.

Elijah, God's man, knew he was in a war, fighting for the minds and hearts of the people. He knew that he would have to get them to choose between Baal and Jehovah.

The Lord continues to insist that a choice be made. We must choose between what is real and what is counterfeit. It is time for all believers to come off the fence. Either God, through His word, or the Psychic Hotline will provide the direction for life. You can't straddle the fence, the choice is either the Bible or your astrological chart. You can't have both as your source of authority. You must be either hot or cold. (Rev. 3:15) You cannot be "wishy-washy" or double-minded. (James 1:8)

So to help them make up their minds, Elijah called for a contest. God's prophet said to the Israelites that since it was clear that they could not make up their minds, it was best to let the real God prove Himself. Elijah said, "Let the God that answereth by fire be God." (I Kings 18:24)

Elijah laid the ground rules for the contest. He told the prophets of Baal to get a bullock and lay it on an altar. After they had done that, they were to call on Baal to light the fire. After they had taken their chance of proving their god, Elijah was to have a chance to get a bullock, put it on the altar, and call on his God to light his fire. Elijah said that whichever of the two answered by fire, all should accept that one as the one true God.

Elijah made them a deal they could not refuse. The false prophet's god, Baal, was known as the fire god. They had no doubts they would win this contest. One Bible historian wrote that Baal was believed by his followers to be the fire of the sun.

The contest began with the prophets of Baal calling on their god. From early morning until noon, they called on Baal to light the fire. They cried out. They prayed. They begged, but no fire fell. They lost all their decorum by jumping up on the altar itself, but still there was no fire. At noon, Elijah began to mock them. He started teasing them. He baited them, "Holler louder; maybe he is busy on another case. Maybe he is on a coffee break. Maybe he's chilling. Maybe he's asleep." The reaction of the prophets of Baal was only to holler more. Since the screaming didn't bring a response from Baal, the false prophets began cutting themselves with knives, bleeding all over the altar.

Some folks serve the kind of gods that make them suffer. Those who follow the drug god, the alcohol god, the gang god, and the god of corruption always end up suffering. But we believers serve a God who relieves suffering. "Come unto me all ye that labor and are heavy laden, and I will give you rest. Take my yoke upon you and learn of me; for I am meek and lowly in heart: and ye shall find rest unto your souls. For my yoke is easy, and my burden is light." (Matthew 11:28-30)

Several years ago, while working on my doctorate, our entire class spent a few weeks in Jamaica and Haiti studying indigenous religious expressions. We were looking for links between indigenous practices and African religious tradition. While in Haiti we attended a ritual one evening which was held on the outskirts of Port au Prince. For hours the worshipers danced around a fire. They swallowed swords and flung themselves about. The ritual required them to cut off the heads of chickens and sling the blood all around. The entire service was not only gruesome, but I am sure it was painful for the participants. I was glad when the service ended. On arriving back at the bus, all I could say was, "Thank you God for Jesus." It's a joy to know we serve a God who does not require that we abuse ourselves.

What's clear is that the Baal prophets had faith in Baal's power. It is clear that Baal's believer were zealous. We can learn from Baal's prophets that it is possible to have faith in and zeal for that which has no power. Could it be that too many of us have deposited our faith in the wrong stuff? Many have deposited their faith in money, and there is nothing wrong with having money, but money will not save you. African-Americans, like all people, need education, but academic degrees are not holy. I am proud of my blackness. When God made us, He did not make a mistake. I can say like David, "I am fearfully and wonderfully made. (Psalms 139:14) But I am clear that my blackness is not divine in and of itself. We need a real God!

At evening time Elijah declared it was time for the real God to demonstrate His power. "And it came to pass at the time of the offering of the evening sacrifice, that Elijah the prophet came near, and said, Lord God of Abraham, Isaac, and of Israel, let it be known this day that thou art God in Israel, and that I am thy servant, and that I have done all these things at thy word." (I Kings 18:36) Elijah explained that they had given Baal all day long to prove himself, but now it was time for them to give the Lord a chance. What

Elijah said to Israel, I say to you, "It's time for us to give God His chance in our lives."

Elijah demonstrated what we ought to do when we need a response from the Lord. He prayed. "Hear me, O Lord, hear me, that this people may know that thou are the Lord God, and that thou hast turned their hearts back again." (I Kings 18:37) With these words, "The fire of God fell." Oh my brothers and my sisters, God can light your fire!

When the people saw that the Lord had answered by fire, they returned to Him. They experienced revival. They fell on their faces; they repented, and they worshiped. They said excitedly, "The Lord He is God; the Lord He is God." After the Lord lights your fire, you ought to make some response. When He lights your fire, does the miraculous, heals your body, protects your sanity, forgives your sins, saves your marriage, helps you raise your children, gives you a promotion on that job, delivers you from the clutch of the enemy, liberates you from low self-esteem, puts joy back in your life, and puts food on your table—you ought to do something about it.

When worshipers gather in their churches, the purpose ought not be to encourage the Lord to do something more. Worship and praise ought to go up because the Lord has already done something for which we are grateful. God has been constantly lighting fires. We should gather with hearts of joy and appreciation to tell the Lord, "Thank you, for lighting our fires."

Whatever cold, dead, defeated, lifeless place there may be in your life, I want to remind you that the one true and living God is able to light your fire. We ought not be tempted to turn to inadequate substitutes when real power is available to us. God can, and He has proven himself time and time again. This God of ours can defend Himself against any and all opposing forces. He is willing and able to be God in our homes, in our schools, on our jobs, and in our churches.

Elijah said that our God sent the fire on Mount Carmel. The disciples testified that on the day of Pentecost, He sent the fire of the Holy Spirit to the upper room and lit their fire. But the best news is that His fire is still available today for you. Whatever you are going through, whatever challenges are confronting you, remember your greatest resource. Get those hands up, throw that head back, and in faith cry out toward heaven. "Lord, light my fire!" "Lord, send the fire." "Lord, thank you for the fire!"

GOD CAN

Help You See Beyond What You See

And Elijah said unto Ahab, Get thee up, eat and drink; for there is a sound of abundance of rain. So Ahab went up to eat and drink. And Elijah went to the top of Carmel; and he cast himself down upon the earth, and put his face between his knees, and said to his servant, Go up now, look toward the sea. And he went up, and looked, and said, There is nothing. And he said, Go again seven times.

—*I Kings 18:41 - 43*

GOD CAN

Help You See Beyond What You See

To see in the natural order requires physical perception, sociological sensitivity, and psychological balance. But to see beyond what you see requires spiritual vision. What is spiritual vision? It is intelligence that is divinely shared with men and women of God. It is seeing reality before it concretizes, or as Paul put it, "It is calling those things that are not as though they were." (Romans 4:17) Spiritual vision is the means by which God shares Himself. Eschatologically speaking, it is being allowed a glimpse of the eschaton. Rev. Dr. James Forbes of the Riverside Church in New York states it this way, "It is being allowed to tiptoe over to the edge of the end of time and see God as the winner."

Spiritual vision allows one to see, hear, feel, or experience God and what He is going to do. Every believer ought to have a vision of what the Lord desires for his or her own life. Once we are able to see the Lord's intention for us, we must also struggle to live in obedience to that vision. We must be able to make the same confession as Paul when he told Agrippa that he was not disobedient to his heavenly vision. (Acts 26:19)

If there was ever a time in the history of humanity when the church was needed, that time is now. There is evidence all over the world of divided, broken, confused, and troubled humanity. God's people with their God-given visions need to step forward to help the helpless. What could be said generally of the peoples of the world can be said of African-Americans most specifically. Over half of our children live in poverty. Gang violence, drug addiction, suicide, divorce, and single parenthood are all on the rise. All across this country there is a growing mean-spirited conservatism that is threatening to turn back the hands on the clock of progress. The prevailing political voices seem to think that the best solution to the problems of the poor is to hire more policemen and build more jails. Evidence of this is seen in the construction of new prisons all over this country. The penal business is now registered on the New York Stock Exchange. Now it is "good business" to keep our prisons filled. We need believers with a vision to tell the politicians that the incarceration of the poor is not the answer.

There should be no greater advocate for the poor and the weak than the body of Christ. There is so much potential power in the African-American church. There is such brilliance, talent, giftedness, skill, charisma, and ability in the Black Church. What seems to be missing is vision.

Can the believers, can the leaders of the church, see beyond what they can see? I know there are visions for new ministries, visions for more tithe-paying members, visions for television broadcasts, visions for new church buildings. But are there visions for empowerment, liberation, and individual and societal salvation? Can anybody see God's plan? Is anybody looking or listening? Is there an Elijah in the House?

God's prophet Elijah found himself living under pressure. Elijah' s pressure was rooted in the fact that he was attempting to lead a people that believed that following the Lord was not socially acceptable. The King and Queen were devoted to Baal. The prophets of Baal seemed to outnumber the prophets of the Lord. Jehovah was cramping their style. He was to demanding. Worshiping Him was just not fashionable. So they began to make up their own faith saying, "drink, eat, and worship, and act the way you want to act." This free mode of behavior caused Israel to decide that it was all right to get a new god, one that was more socially acceptable, a god that would give them higher social status.

Most Israelites did not feel they had left the Lord. They just wanted a wider selection. They wanted enough freedom to practice a kind of "buffet" religion. We can understand—a little Muhammad and a little Jesus, a little Jesus and a little astrology, a little psychic hotline and a little Jesus. There is absolutely no biblical support for this sort of syncretism. Joshua admonished Israel, "Choose you this day whom you shall serve." (Joshua 24:15)

James records that the Lord led Elijah to pray that the clouds would dry up, and that there would be no rain. (James 5:17) And what a major drought there was: no rain, famine, cattle dead, crops failed, brooks dried up, grass withered, and death was the order of the day. There were no exceptions. If God is excluded a drought will come to your home, your marriage, your job, your finances, your health, and your church. But when the Israeli people saw the mighty hand of God, they repented. When they saw that God could answer by fire, but Baal could not, they repented. When they saw that God could turn the water off and Baal couldn't turn it back on, they repented. When they saw that God had the power, and Baal had none, they repented. After they repented, the Lord was ready to send the rain.

Oh, my friends, good things follow repentance. "If we confess our sins, He is faithful and just to forgive us our sins, and to cleanse us from all unrighteousness." (I John 1:9) After the people repented, the Lord gave Elijah a vision of an abundance of rain. Once Elijah received the vision from the Lord, it became his reality. God's vision is not imagination. It is not simply a good idea, but it is reality. When you have been given vision by the Lord, you ought to have enough faith to walk around in it. That vision ought to be the driving force in your life. It should provide for you direction for how you live your life daily.

About fifteen years ago, I was at a retreat with my ministerial staff at Bethel A.M.E. Church in Baltimore, where I served as the senior pastor. While I was at the altar, the Lord gave me a vision for a Labor Day sunrise service. I saw that at the service we were to do something for the unemployed. The Lord showed me that we were to provide jobs for them and provide brand-new back-to-school shoes for their children. I could see every detail, and when I got up from the altar, I did not share an idea with my staff, but I shared reality. It was that reality that became the mission focus for our church.

Elijah, who had embraced the reality in his vision, told King Ahab, "I can hear the abundance of rain." (I Kings 18:41) Ahab could not hear it, nor could he see it, for he had not had the vision. Elijah could see beyond what he could see, because he had the vision. The visionless Ahab could only see a drought. He could only see what he could see. He continued business as usual, but Elijah, the man with a vision, went up to the top of Mount Carmel to pray. Elijah went up.

If you are to see beyond what you see, you have to go up. You must go up in your altitude to an attitude that grows out of faith in the goodness of God. This kind of attitude finds the believer living and looking up. As Isaiah declared: "But they that wait upon the Lord shall mount up with wings as eagles; they shall run and not be weary; and they shall walk and not faint." (Isaiah 40:3)

If you are to see beyond what you see, you will also have to have a disciplined prayer life. Visions do not come automatically with seminary degrees, or with elections to church office, or with pastoral appointments, or with a call from the pulpit committee. Visions come from the Lord. When we see Elijah on his knees at the top of Mount Carmel, it must remind us that those who appear publicly for God must spend private time with God. Candidates for heavenly vision must spend quality time with their ears and their hearts turned upward.

After Elijah had prayed, he sent his servant up to see what he could see. Servants of the kingdom are still being sent up. Pastors, evangelists, missionaries, Christian education workers, youth workers, and outreach ministers are being sent up, and the Lord wants to know what do you, or your ministry, see?

Elijah's servant said, "I see nothing." In other words, all the servant saw was the same old thing. We ought to pay very close attention to the prophet's servant, for he was moving through a necessary process. Before you can see beyond, you must first see what is at hand. You have to see the drought before you can see the rain. Derrick Bell, in his book, *Faces at the Bottom of the Well*, describes the devastating racism that is still at work in the United States. It is ugly, and we cannot deny its presence. The followers of the Lord

Jesus Christ must see troubled marriages, dysfunctional families, a growing underclass, gang violence, escalating suicide, homicides, rape, and drug trafficing and addiction, before we can see the reality of the vision. Open your eyes and see the many churches with declining memberships. Churches with no youth, no males, and no joy. We must see the churches that seem no longer to have a burden for the poor. Churches that offer to their members comfortable pews, air-conditioned facilities, but no crosses to bear. We must see churches that fight to stop abortions, while killing aid to dependent children. We must see believers who preach the sanctity of life and simultaneously vote for the death penalty. We must see humanity's inhumanity to humanity. If we do not see the social and spiritual drought, we cannot minister, we cannot preach, and we will not even know what to pray.

So Elijah's servant could see the drought. His problem was the drought was the only thing he could see. The servant could not see beyond what he could see. Elijah continued in prayer and instructed his servant to go back and look again. Elijah could see beyond what he could see. He had a vision. And because he wanted to share the vision, he told the servant to go back again and again and to look up. We must not spend all of our time looking down at our problems. We must look up for heaven's solutions.

Finally, on the seventh time, the servant looked up and saw a sign of the coming rain. What he saw was a little cloud no bigger than a person's hand.

I believe in the Black community we are struggling to see a little cloud of hope. The African-American community is going through a difficult period. It sounds like a cliché, but it is true. The poor are getting poorer. There are more African-American males in jail than in college, and forty-nine percent of our homes are being led by females. As Myles Munroe has written in his book, *Understand Your Potential*, too many of us are allowing ourselves to be seen as junk that others are free to throw away. In this nation where racism still exists, and many states have not demonstrated any track record in dealing equitably with minorities and/or the poor, we wonder about the little cloud of hope. We see national leaders calling for the federal government to extricate itself from those concerns and turn them over to the states to handle, while at the same time, several states have moved for the dismantling of Affirmative Action programs. Affirmative Action programs were instituted to make the "playing field" level. But all are aware that all the statistical data confirms that the field is not yet level. For most African-Americans these are the signs of a major drought.

But I see something else. Look up, for every now and then I see a little cloud of hope. I see a husband and wife opening their home to adopt five community children who had been labeled "at risk." I see a school teacher giving up her free afternoons to tutor students to prepare them for college entrance. I see churches involving themselves in economic development ventures in order to provide jobs for the unemployed.

I see preachers teaching lessons of liberation and empowerment from God's word. I see the drought, but I thank God that I can see beyond what I can see. I can see my Jesus with outstretched hands declaring, "I am with you always." (Matthew 28:20)

Look again. Can't you see it—it's going to rain! Our drought will come to an end. Our mess will give way to God's miracles. Our people can begin to open their hands and their hearts to receive heaven's outpouring. Our churches will receive in full measure the rain of the anointing. I promise you, if you keep looking up, you too will see it. For already, "Mine eyes have seen the glory of the coming of the Lord, He is trampling out the vintage where the grapes of wrath are stored; He hath loosed the fateful lighting of His terrible swift sword; His truth is marching on. Glory! Glory! Hallelujah." Only those who let God help them see beyond what they can see will be able to see it and will shout, Glory! Glory! Hallelujah!

GOD CAN
Enable You

And the hand of the Lord was on Elijah; and he girded up his loins, and ran before Ahab to the entrance of Jezreel.

—I Kings 18:46

GOD CAN
Enable You

One of the major tricks of Satan is to convince us that our dilemmas in life are hopeless. Satan wants to convince us that sickness is unto death, that a mistake is irreparable, that the enemy cannot be defeated, that we will never overcome our weaknesses, and that we will never be victorious over the challenges that confront us in life. But we need not be victim's of Satan's tricks. We must always remember that Satan is a liar. (Rev. 12:9)

Satan works full time to convince us that we do not have the victory. As a bishop, I have seen many ministries that are bound because they have believed the lie that they cannot grow. Some of these churches are located in communities where unchurched people live all around them, yet they will refer to themselves as the "faithful few." These church members can be heard saying, "People don't have time for God anymore" or "The streets are so bad people will not come out to church." Some church members go so far as to say, "We're so old now no one wants to have anything to do with us." Believers must stop that talk and be determined not to be defeated by the lies of Satan. God has already declared us conquerors. (Romans 8:37) As believers, we always have a choice when faced with life's dilemmas. We have a choice about what we will say, which way we will go, and what we will do. When we find ourselves in the moment of crisis, the question is "Who will we believe?" Will we believe Satan, who is a deceiver, or will we believe the Bible, which is the word of God? We must not believe Satan, whose very name "diabolos" in Greek means, adversary, false accuser, and slanderer. It is imperative that we believe the Lord whose love for us is so great that there is nothing that can separate us from him. No matter the obstacle, no matter the challenge, the believer must live in the awareness that in the presence of our strong God we cannot be defeated. We must keep in mind that in the Lord our abilities are boundless. In Christ there are no ceilings or walls. There is nothing that can keep us down. This is the message that must be proclaimed to African-American youth. Far too many are living below their potential. Far too many are living without hope. Early pregnancies, gang participation, and substance abuse are all signs that many are settling for a life beneath God's plan for their lives. In Christ Jesus, we can be and ought to be "sky-walkers."

This is the assurance that claimed my attention when I read I Kings 18:46. "And the hand of the Lord

was on Elijah; and he girded up his loins and ran before Ahab to the entrance of Jezreel." Elijah was em-
powered. God enabled him. God overshadowed Him
with His Spirit. No wonder Elijah could gird up his
loins and run before Ahab's chariot. Repeatedly in the
chapters 17 and 18 of I Kings, we have seen Elijah being used in supernatural ways. These chapters teach us
that prayers on the lips of a believer result in being en-
dowed with great power. In chapter 17, Elijah prayed
and the heavens went on strike in agreement with his
prayer. In chapter 18, we saw him praying again. This
time he prays for rain and the flood gates of heaven
open wide.

Elijah, in chapter 18, sent word to Ahab that he
should hurry home to the palace before the coming
rains flooded out the roads. Isn't it something that
Elijah's prayer-answering God has the power to go from
drought to a flood in the matter of minutes. What we
have discovered is that the same God who lit Elijah's
fire on Mount Carmel is the same God who backed up
his prayer for rain. He is also the same God who enabled Elijah to run before the King's chariot all the way
to Jezreel.

Elijah ran before Ahab's chariot. Reason demands
to know how a man could run in front of horses. We
have overlooked the answer, "And the hand of the Lord
was on Elijah." The Bible expressed the concept of the
workings of God's power in different ways: "The hand
of the Lord," "the spirit of the Lord," "the presence of
the Lord," "the grace of the Lord," "the might of the

Lord," and "the authority of the Lord." All of these phrases mean—God can enable you!

Those who understand that they have a need to be enabled by God ought to pay close attention to verse forty-six. In this verse, we uncover the source of our liberation, our healing, our deliverance. Empowerment comes from the hand of God. Jesus understood that this is what made His last utterance on Calvary's cross appropriate, "Father into Thy hands I commend my spirit." (Luke 23:46)

It doesn't matter how gifted you are, you cannot enable yourself. Humanists may teach you that you are self-sufficient, but I want you to know that you need God on your side. No government, or court, or political party can enable you. No ideology, elected official, or charismatic leader can save you. But Paul wrote that the Lord "is able to do exceedingly, abundantly above all that we ask or think." (Ephesians 3:20) It was out of the reality of this awesome truth that we hear Elijah testify, "The hand of the Lord was upon me."

Yes, the Lord is more than able to enable. The Lord is able to do His part, but we are responsible to do our part. The text says that the believer must do something. Elijah said, "I girded up my loins, and ran." During the time when this narrative occurred, men wore long flowing robes. If one intended to do some serious running, all encumbrances had to be put aside. So Elijah pulled up his robe from around his ankles to waist level and tied it in place—he girded up his loins.

If we believers are going to seriously run the race
of life, we are going to have to get some stuff out of
the way. Pride, low self-esteem, and negative attitudes
must go. Crippling traditions, non-supportive friends,
defeatist language from our own mouths must go. All
of these encumbrances must be removed so that we
might run with Christ.

When the Lord laid His hands on Elijah, he was
blessing the prophet in two ways. First, the Lord was
giving his prophet supernatural strength. To be able to
run successfully on the highway of life, the Lord must
enable you.

But Satan is seeking to tell people differently. The
poor and the oppressed have been told repeatedly that
they can make it with the right education, or the right
job, or the right legislation. But I submit that what one
needs can be found only in the hand of Lord. The Lord
is able to provide that man and that woman in need
with physical, emotional, and strength. Whatever race
or trial is before you, I want you to know that only
the Lord can enable you to run with horses.

When the Lord laid His hands on Elijah, he was
not only giving him strength, but he was also bestow-
ing on the prophet divine guidance. By running ahead
of the King, Elijah was demonstrating great wisdom.
Elijah was a man who had recently asked God to light
his fire, and God responded by lighting his fire. This
is the same man who prayed and God shut the heavens in response to his prayer. Yet, we see this great and
powerful man running like a lowly footman before the

chariot of an earthly king. When God enables you, you can be secure enough to be a servant to others. Elijah, through his humility, was attempting to win the King to faith in his God. His act of humility did not diminish His stature. When the Lord enables you, you don't have to fight for image, position, or title, for the Lord Himself will make room for you. The job of the believer is to line up with the will of the Lord and make himself available to God's touch. We have races to run. We have battles to fight. We have mountains to climb, problems to solve, victories to win, and enemies to overcome. But all we need is the Lord to lay His hands on us.

It is my prayer that before you put this book down, you will be convinced that you, as a believer, have a great resource available to you. And the treasure is none other than the great arm of the Lord. The Lord is able! Let this truth permeate your soul. God can enable you!

As you go through life and confront trails and tests, don't panic or give up, know that "God Can Back You Up," that "God Can Use Anything," that "God Can Multiply by Subtracting," that "God Can Light Your Fire," that "God Can Help You See Beyond What You See," and that "God Can Enable You."

For book orders contact:

Bishop John Ministries
4347 South Hampton Rd., Suite 245
Dallas, Texas 75232
Telephone: 214-333-2632
FAX: 214-333-1960